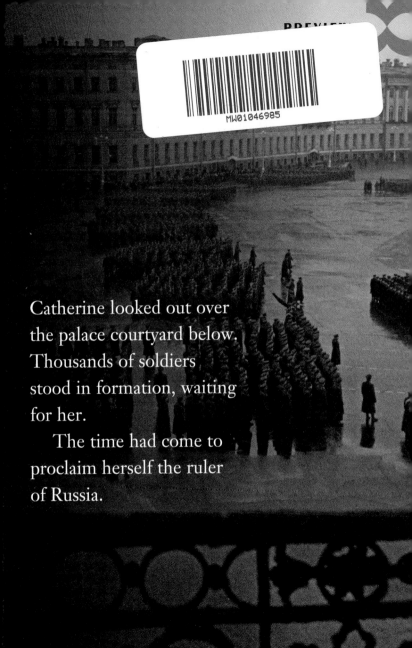

Catherine looked out over
the palace courtyard below.
Thousands of soldiers
stood in formation, waiting
for her.

The time had come to
proclaim herself the ruler
of Russia.

The Plot

The pieces were in place. Catherine had the loyalty of the Imperial Guard. They were the personal protectors of Tsar Peter III—the current ruler of Russia. She had sent messengers to tell the Russian people that Peter had betrayed them. Next she would send a message to Peter, demanding that he give up the throne.

Taking Charge

Catherine stepped out of the palace.
Thousands of eyes followed her as she
strode down the steps, her long hair flowing
around her face.

A roar went up from the crowd.
With every step, she claimed the palace
as her own.

A Tsarina Is Born

Finally, after years of planning, Catherine was seizing the throne of Russia—from her own husband.

The Question

How did Catherine manage to gain
so much power? And why is it hard for
leaders to live up to their ideals?

PREVIEW PHOTOS

PAGE 1: A military parade at the Winter Palace in St. Petersburg

PAGES 2-3: Catherine is welcomed by religious leaders at Kazan Cathedral on the day she proclaimed herself empress.

PAGES 4-5: Surrounded by Russian soldiers, Catherine takes an oath to become empress.

Book Design: Red Herring Design/NYC **Photo Credits:** Photographs © 2012: Art Resource, NY: 28 (Maurice-Quentin de La Tour/Musee d'Art et d'Histoire/bpk, Berlin), 29 right (Erich Lessing/Institut et Musee Voltaire, Geneva), 29 left (Réunion des Musées Nationaux), 45 top left (Alexandre Roslin/Scala/White Images); 26 (The New York Public Library); Bridgeman Art Library International Ltd., London/New York: 15 (Art Gallery of Taganrog, Russia), 41 (Jean-Baptiste Bayot/Edouard Jean-Marie Hostein/Pushkin Museum, Moscow), 17 top left (Fitzwilliam Museum, University of Cambridge, UK), 18 (Georg Cristoph Grooth/Odessa Fine Arts Museum, Ukraine), 12 (Georg Cristoph Grooth/Tretyakov Gallery, Moscow), 24 (Luigi Premazzi/Hermitage, St. Petersburg), 17 top right (Private Collection/The Stapleton Collection); Corbis Images/Alfredo Dagli Orti/The Art Archive: 38; Getty Images: 1 (Glow Images), 43 (Imagno); Mark Summers: cover; NEWSCOM/akg-images: 30 (Russian Picture Service), 10, 17 bottom, 33 top, 45 top right; North Wind Picture Archives: 40; ShutterStock, Inc.: 42 (Ruth Black), back cover foreground (Michael Drager), 33 bottom (Olga Miltsova), 44 frame, 45 frame (NinaMalyna); The Art Archive/Picture Desk: 21 (Alfredo Dagli Orti/Russian Historical Museum Moscow), 44 right (Gianni Dagli Orti/Musée du Château de Versailles); The Granger Collection, New York/Stefano Torelli: 34; The Image Works: 13 (akg-images), 36, 45 bottom left (Mary Evans Picture Library), 8 (RIA Novosti/TopFoto), 32 (RIA Novosti/Topham), 37, 45 bottom right (Roger-Viollet); The State Hermitage Museum, St. Petersburg/Photos by Vladimir Terebenin, Leonard Kheifets, Yuri Molodkovets: 2, 3, 4, 5, 16, 44 left.

Maps by XNR Productions, Inc.

Library of Congress Cataloging-in-Publication Data
Rozett, Louise.
Ice queen : Catherine the Great seizes power in Russia / Louise Rozett.
p. cm. — (Xbooks)
Includes bibliographical references and index.
ISBN-13: 978-0-545-32946-0
ISBN-10: 0-545-32946-9
1. Catherine II, Empress of Russia, 1729-1796—Juvenile literature. 2. Empresses—Russia—Biography—Juvenile literature. 3. Russia—History—Catherine II, 1762-1796—Juvenile literature. I. Title.
DK170.R69 2012   947'.063092—dc23
2011023335

ICE QUEEN

Catherine the Great Seizes Power in Russia

LOUISE ROZETT

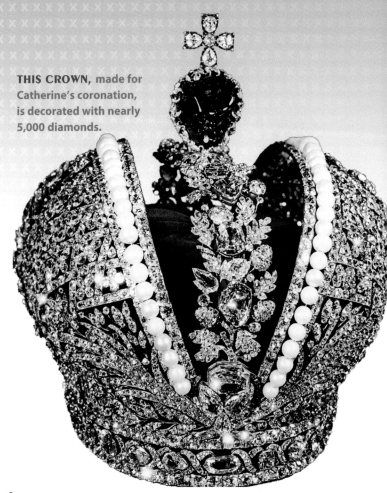

THIS CROWN, made for Catherine's coronation, is decorated with nearly 5,000 diamonds.

TABLE OF CONTENTS

Groomed for Greatness

A mother proposes her daughter as a bride.

Long before she was known as Catherine, Princess Sophie Friederike Auguste had been groomed for greatness. She came from the grim German city of Stettin, far from the big palaces of Europe. But Sophie's mother, Princess Johanna, was determined to find a grand royal marriage for her daughter.

Servants hovered over Sophie. Tutors schooled her in religion, dance, music, and languages. Bright and chatty, Sophie took to her lessons well. Before she turned five, she could read French, the language of Europe's elite.

Johanna took her little girl to royal parties in nearby states. Sophie felt right at home among Europe's princes and princesses.

In 1740 Johanna had her ten-year-old daughter introduced to a 12-year-old duke named Peter Ulrich. Sophie found him to be dull and childish. He would only talk about soldiers and war. But he was next in line for the throne of Russia. That was more than enough to make him a desirable husband.

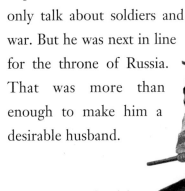

YOUNG PETER, Russia's future tsar, was one of the most eligible bachelors in the world. He was also immature and dull.

Princess Sophie was confident that she deserved to be Peter's wife. "Of all the matches proposed," she boasted in her diary, "I am the most brilliant."

A few years later, Sophie and her mother set out for St. Petersburg, the capital of Russia. They traveled the 800 miles through deep snow in a horse-drawn sleigh. If the empress of Russia approved of Sophie, Sophie would become Peter's wife.

Shifting Alliances

In her quest to marry Peter, Sophie had become a pawn in an international struggle for power. Her home city of Stettin was part of the newly expanding

Kingdom of Prussia. The kingdom included much of present-day Germany and parts of Poland. Prussia's king, Frederick II, was preparing for war with his archenemy, Austria.

Frederick was eager to increase his power by forming an alliance, or partnership, with Russia. A Prussian wife for Peter could be just what Frederick needed to make the alliance work.

That was exactly what many people in Russia feared. Austria and Russia had been allies for many years. Powerful people in Russia bitterly opposed the idea of Peter risking that alliance by marrying a Prussian. Aware that they might be in danger, Johanna and Sophie made their journey in secret.

Even if Sophie arrived safely, more dangers would be waiting for her. She would have to charm Peter's aunt, the Empress Elizabeth. And Elizabeth had a reputation for violence. It was rumored that Elizabeth had cut out the tongue of a beautiful countess who had gossiped about her.

What would Elizabeth do to Sophie if she decided the young woman was not right for Peter?

ELIZABETH HAD BECOME empress of Russia by overthrowing her infant cousin. Then she made her Swedish nephew Peter her heir to the Russian throne.

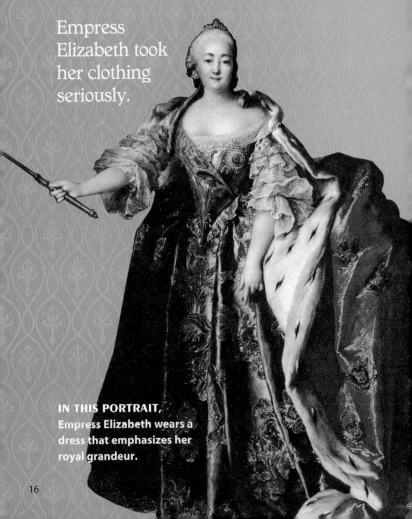

Fabulous Fashionista

Empress Elizabeth took her clothing seriously.

IN THIS PORTRAIT, Empress Elizabeth wears a dress that emphasizes her royal grandeur.

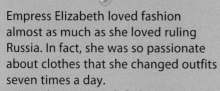

Empress Elizabeth loved fashion almost as much as she loved ruling Russia. In fact, she was so passionate about clothes that she changed outfits seven times a day.

Her obsession with fashion extended to the ladies in her court. Their clothing was stamped with special ink so they could never wear the same gown twice. No lady was allowed to outshine the empress, however. When one woman's gown caught Elizabeth's eye, she supposedly cut it up with scissors—while the woman was wearing it.

ELIZABETH OWNED 15,000 dresses and thousands of pairs of shoes. And she insisted on French-made clothing. This earned her the nickname "the Russian lady in French heels."

ELIZABETH WAS fashionable from an early age. In this famous childhood portrait, Elizabeth (with blonde hair) is wearing a magnificent gold dress.

2

Catherine!

A new name. A new title. And a new husband.

When Princess Sophie and her mother arrived in St. Petersburg, Empress Elizabeth received them dressed in a shimmering silver gown. Diamonds glittered in the empress's hair. As Elizabeth scrutinized the young princess, Sophie curtsied before her. When Sophie rose, the empress kissed her.

Sophie had passed her first test.

Settling in, Sophie dutifully learned the ways of her

new country. She studied Russia's culture, language, and religion. In 1744 she converted to the official religion of the country and joined the Russian Orthodox Church.

A New Name

When the ceremony was over, Princess Sophie was re-christened. From now on she would be known as Catherine, in memory of Elizabeth's mother.

Catherine's dedication to Russia deeply touched Elizabeth. Soon the empress announced that Catherine and Peter would marry.

On August 21, 1745, 16-year-old Catherine stood through three agonizing hours of prayers and sermons. She wore an enormous crown and a wedding gown that weighed nearly half as much as she did. When it was over, Catherine had a new title—Grand Duchess of All of the Russias.

Catherine had finally married into one of the most powerful families in Europe. And yet her life was full of sadness.

Why? Because her husband informed her that he did not love her. He spent his time playing with toy soldiers and chasing other women. On some days Peter made Catherine dress like a soldier and stand guard outside his room for hours. And once he showed her a dead pet rat that he had hanged by its neck for being a "bad soldier."

Alone

Even Catherine's hard-won ally Elizabeth turned against her. Now that Catherine had married into the family, the empress started to see her as a threat. What would prevent Catherine from plotting to steal the throne? Elizabeth assigned spies to keep a close watch on the duchess.

Catherine had a grand title and a powerful family. Yet she was completely alone, 800 miles from home.

PETER WAS OBSESSED with the military. But he had more experience playing with toy soldiers than fighting in real battles.

Mother Russia

In the 1740s, it was a vast empire.

GREAT BRITAIN

N

FRANCE

SWEDEN

ANHALT-ZERBST

A

Berlin • Stettin

PRUSSIA

Baltic Sea

Oranienbaum C

St. Petersburg

B

AUSTRIA

Kiev • Dnieper R. • Moscow

UKRAINE

RUSSIA

Aegean Sea

Crimea

OTTOMAN EMPIRE

Black Sea

Volga R.

Ural R.

Mediterranean Sea

Caspian Sea

Aral Sea

WHAT WERE THE RUSSIAN PEOPLE LIKE?

About 19 million people lived in Russia. About 50,000 were rich nobles who owned their own land. The rest were poor serfs who were forced to work for the nobles.

WHAT WAS IT LIKE IN RUSSIA?

There were several magnificent cities in Russia. But most of the country was undeveloped. The nobles had vast wealth. But the serfs owned nothing and suffered under tyrannical rulers.

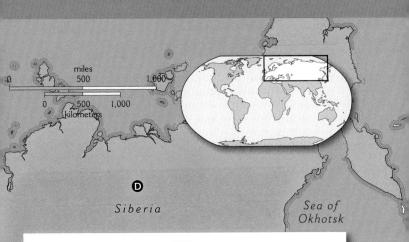

miles

0   500   1,000

0   500   1,000
kilometers

Ⓓ

Siberia

Sea of Okhotsk

KEY

Ⓐ Princess Sophie (later called Catherine the Great) was born in Stettin in 1729.

Ⓑ Sophie arrived in the Russian capital in 1744, hoping to marry Peter, heir to the Russian throne.

Ⓒ In 1762 Catherine seized the throne of Russia from her husband, Tsar Peter III. Peter was murdered a few weeks later.

Ⓓ In 1790 Catherine exiled Alexander Radishchev to Siberia after he wrote that the serfs should be freed.

Lands Catherine Acquired:

░░░ Territory taken from the Ottoman Empire

░░░ Territory taken from Poland

Map is a Lambert Azimuthal equal-area projection, not a Mercator projection.

3

Enlightenment

Catherine turns to books— and a new friend.

Catherine was trapped in a velvet prison. She had every luxury under the sun. But she had almost no one to talk to. To fight off her loneliness, she buried herself in writing and reading. She continued the journal she had kept since childhood. And she studied the exciting new ideas that were sweeping through Europe.

In France, a new group of writers were challenging the authority of kings, queens, and priests. They encouraged ordinary people to think for themselves. They based their beliefs on reason instead of tradition. And they pushed for new rights such as freedom of speech and religion.

Catherine absorbed the ideas of this new movement, which became known as the Enlightenment. She knew that someday she'd rule Russia with Peter. She thought that at least one of them should govern wisely—and she knew it wouldn't be him.

Alexei Bestuzhev

More than ten lonely years went by. Catherine hungered for political power. At balls and other gatherings she reached out to important and

ALEXEI BESTUZHEV, Elizabeth's foreign-policy adviser, made a secret alliance with Catherine.

influential people. One person she became close to was Elizabeth's foreign-policy adviser, Alexei Bestuzhev. Bestuzhev wanted Catherine, not Peter, to take the throne after Elizabeth died.

When Elizabeth discovered that Bestuzhev had been counseling Catherine, she went crazy with rage. In 1758 she had Bestuzhev arrested and charged with treason—the crime of betraying one's country.

Performance of a Lifetime

Catherine knew she was in grave danger. She had to ask Elizabeth for forgiveness. But when she arrived in Elizabeth's chambers, Peter was standing next to the empress, smirking.

Catherine made her plea to the empress. She insisted that she had never been disloyal and apologized for corresponding with Bestuzhev. Peter interrupted her, calling her a liar. But Peter's outbursts annoyed Elizabeth, and the empress eventually took Catherine's side.

When Catherine left the chamber she was relieved to be alive—but determined to keep making alliances.

A Bold New World

Meet a few of the thinkers behind the Enlightenment.

JEAN-JACQUES ROUSSEAU: THE PHILOSOPHER (1712-1778)

Rousseau is best known for inventing the term "Social Contract." Rousseau claimed that people have an unspoken contract with their rulers. According to that contract, the people agree to be ruled, and in exchange the government protects their liberty, property, and happiness. If the rulers don't fulfill their part of the contract, the people have the right to overthrow them and choose new rulers.

DENIS DIDEROT: THE EDITOR (1713-1784)

Diderot was the editor of the *Encyclopédie*, a 35-volume collection of writings about all the new ideas of the time. Before it was even finished, the *Encyclopédie* was banned in France. So Catherine invited Diderot to Russia to complete his work.

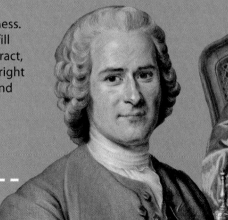

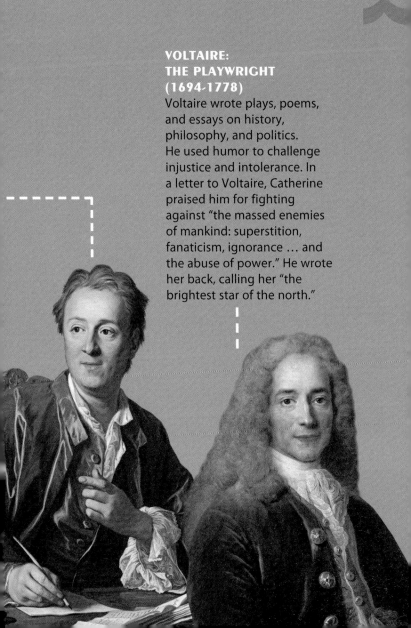

**VOLTAIRE:
THE PLAYWRIGHT
(1694-1778)**
Voltaire wrote plays, poems,
and essays on history,
philosophy, and politics.
He used humor to challenge
injustice and intolerance. In
a letter to Voltaire, Catherine
praised him for fighting
against "the massed enemies
of mankind: superstition,
fanaticism, ignorance … and
the abuse of power." He wrote
her back, calling her "the
brightest star of the north."

4

The Final Obstacle

Catherine is one step
closer to the throne.

In 1760 Catherine made an important new friend. He was a dashing soldier named Gregory Orlov. Catherine had spotted him from a palace window. He was the most handsome man she'd ever seen. Orlov was an officer in the Imperial Guard and a war hero. He and his four brothers, also Imperial Guard officers, had the loyalty of hundreds of soldiers. That made Orlov more than just attractive. It made him a powerful ally.

Catherine began a romance with Orlov a few weeks after meeting him.

By 1761 Empress Elizabeth was gravely ill. Peter prepared to take the throne. Catherine knew that she couldn't survive Peter's rule—and Russia couldn't either. She decided to intervene, with the help of Orlov and his brothers. There was just one small problem.

GREGORY ORLOV hated Peter and was a natural ally for Catherine.

Catherine was pregnant with Orlov's child.

If Peter found out, he would send her away—or worse. Catherine hid her pregnancy from all but a few trusted servants. She prayed that Peter would be too self-involved to notice.

Peter in Power

In January 1762 Elizabeth died, surrounded by priests and servants. Everyone in attendance knelt before Peter, their new ruler. But Peter barely seemed affected by the death of the woman who had given him everything. Catherine stood by silently. She knew that Peter would not rule for long.

During his first months as tsar, Peter made enemies all across Russia. He seized property from the Russian Orthodox Church, angering members of the church. He enraged the military by making peace with Prussia. It was as if he was playing right into Catherine's hands.

In the meantime, Catherine's due date neared. In April, she and a trusted servant came up with a plan to distract Peter while she gave birth. The servant set a fire outside the palace. Peter, who loved fires, ran outside to watch. The baby was born, bundled up, and sent to the countryside to be raised by a servant. Catherine was now in a position to seize the throne. All she had to do was find the perfect moment.

CATHERINE KNEW that a fire would distract Peter.

5

Empress Catherine

"Little Mother, he is no more!"

Catherine spent the summer of 1762 at a palace west of St. Petersburg. She waited anxiously for word from the Orlovs that it was time to seize the throne. Finally, one morning, Catherine awakened to the booming voice of Alexis Orlov.

"We must go!" he announced urgently.

A lieutenant in the Imperial Guard had been arrested. Orlov feared that the lieutenant would be tortured until he revealed the plot.

The time to strike was now—or never.

Her Majesty

Thousands of supporters followed Catherine through St. Petersburg as her carriage made its way to the palace. They shouted "Catherine! Our Little Mother Catherine!"

Catherine's troops secured the palace as she composed a message to be sent far and wide. Peter was a faithless betrayer, she wrote. She was seizing the throne to protect the people and their empire.

Inside the palace, Catherine changed into the uniform of a Russian soldier to show her commitment to the military. She prepared to address her troops. Taking a deep breath, she strode down the palace steps.

WHEN PETER heard that Catherine (left, wearing a military uniform) was trying to overthrow him, he said: "That woman is capable of anything!"

Her message was clear: Peter was no longer in command of the army or the state.

Surrender

At the base of the steps, Catherine jumped on a white horse and rode off. She was followed by nearly 14,000 loyal soldiers.

Peter had taken refuge at Oranienbaum, a royal estate near St. Petersburg. Catherine

TSAR PETER III is killed. Later many people suspected that Catherine had ordered his murder.

convinced Peter's guardsmen to surrender without a fight. Deserted by the last of his troops, Peter surrendered as well. Then he collapsed.

A few weeks later, Catherine received a note from Alexis Orlov. "Little Mother, he is no more!" it read. Peter III of Russia had been murdered—most likely by Orlov himself.

Catherine locked the note away in a drawer. Russia was finally hers.

6

Catherine the Great

The empress leaves a hard-won legacy.

By the time she was 33, Catherine had the power she'd hungered for. She wanted to use it wisely.

Inspired by the Enlightenment, she vowed to bring her country into the modern age. She promised to govern by a system of laws, not by whim as most monarchs did. She called for freedom of speech and the press. And she spoke out in favor of freeing the country's serfs, peasants who were forced to work for wealthy landowners.

Catherine's Reality

In practice, however, Catherine found it hard to live up to her ideals. Her concern for the serfs, for example, was quickly overshadowed by her need to protect herself. Catherine came to realize that she depended on the loyalty of the wealthy landowners. And these landowners relied on the unpaid labor provided by the serfs. So when a serf rebellion broke out in 1773, Catherine sided with the landowners. She suppressed the rebellion and had its leader beheaded.

Denis Diderot, the Enlightenment philosopher, was visiting Catherine at the time of the rebellion. He demanded to know when she was going to free the serfs in Russia. His protests began to annoy Catherine. He was just a writer, she complained in her diary. He did not understand the realities of governing a country.

Catherine ended up doing little to advance the Enlightenment ideal of liberty. But she did support the arts and education. She built schools for boys and girls. And under her guidance, Russian universities became important centers of learning.

She also relaxed censorship rules—but only for a time. In 1789 French revolutionaries overthrew their king. Catherine did not want to be the next ruler to fall. So she banned her friend Voltaire's books. She sent spies to track down revolutionaries across the country. And she exiled a writer to Siberia after he called for freeing the serfs.

CATHERINE FOUNDED the Smolny Cloister to educate the daughters of wealthy nobles.

Catherine ruled for 34 years. She survived longer and accomplished more than anyone thought possible. She was feared and revered until the end. After her death in 1796, she was remembered by a name that reflected her remarkable life: Catherine the Great. ✖

The Last Word

Empress Catherine wanted the final say about her life, so she wrote her own epitaph. But did she tell the whole story?

Here lies Catherine the Second, born in Stettin on April 21, 1729. She came to Russia in 1744 to marry Peter III. At the age of 14, she formed the three-fold project of pleasing her husband, Empress Elizabeth, and the nation. She neglected nothing to succeed in this. Eighteen years of boredom and solitude made her read plenty of books. Arrived on the throne of Russia, she desired its good and sought to procure for her subjects happiness, liberty, and propriety. She forgave easily and hated no one; indulgent, easy to live with, naturally cheerful, with a republican soul and a good heart, she had friends, she found work easy, she liked good society and the arts.

(and the having him killed)

(magically, with the help of a few thousand soldiers)

(except her husband)

(unless you happened to be one of a few million serfs)

FILES

The Real Rulers of St. Petersburg

Catherine's life had all the drama and intrigue of a modern-day reality show. Here are some highlights.

1729 JUST A SMALL-TOWN PRINCESS

Catherine was born Princess Sophie of Anhalt-Zerbst. Her father was a minor prince who governed the port city of Stettin.

1740 BAD DATE

Catherine was ten years old when she first met Peter. She thought he was childish and as dull as a rock. But that didn't matter. One day he would rule Russia. So when she was 16, she married him!

1744 WILD CITY

Catherine traveled to the Russian capital of St. Petersburg to meet her fiancé. Talk about wild! The streets of Catherine's new hometown were lined with grand palaces, but bears and other animals still roamed at night.

1762
WHO'S THE BOSS?
Catherine led thousands of rebellious troops to overthrow her husband. Peter surrendered without a fight, and Catherine became empress of Russia.

1745
EMPRESS-IN-LAW
To marry Peter, Catherine had to win over his aunt, Elizabeth of Russia. The empress was highly intelligent—as well as vain and treacherous.

1762
MURDER OF A TSAR
Peter was assassinated by one of Catherine's supporters. Why? Although Peter had renounced his throne, there was a chance that disloyal nobles might rally around him.

45

RESOURCES

HERE'S A SELECTION OF books AND wEbsiTEs foR moRE iNfoRMATioN AboUT CATHERINE THE GREAT.

What to Read Next

NONFICTION

Hatt, Christine. *Catherine the Great* (Judge for Yourself). Milwaukee: World Almanac Library, 2004.

King, David. *The Enlightenment.* Farmington Hills, MI: Blackbirch Press, 2005.

Raum, Elizabeth. *Catherine the Great.* Chicago: Raintree, 2009.

Strickler, James E. *Russia of the Tsars.* San Diego: Lucent Books, 1998.

Vincent, Zu. *Catherine the Great: Empress of Russia* (A Wicked History). New York: Franklin Watts, 2009.

Whitelaw, Nancy. *Catherine the Great and the Enlightenment in Russia.* Greensboro, NC: Morgan Reynolds, 2005.

FICTION

Gregory, Kristiana. *Catherine: The Great Journey.* New York: Scholastic, 2005.

Websites

Catherine the Great
www.bbc.co.uk/history/historic_figures/catherine_the_great.shtml
BBC History's profile of Catherine the Great.

The Face of Russia
www.pbs.org/weta/faceofrussia/intro.html
This companion website to the PBS series *The Face of Russia* offers an excellent timeline and other resources on Russian history.

The State Hermitage Museum
www.hermitagemuseum.org/html_en/index.html
This is the official website of the State Hermitage Museum in St. Petersburg, Russia, a world-renowned art museum established by Catherine the Great.

ALLIANCE (uh-LYE-uhnss) *noun* an agreement to work together

ARCHENEMY (arch-EN-uh-mee) *noun* the worst enemy

CENSORSHIP (SEN-sur-ship) *noun* a government's banning of books or other expressions of ideas

CHRISTENED (KRISS-ind) *verb* given a Christian name as part of being accepted into a Christian religion

DESOLATE (DESS-uh-luht) *adjective* empty and lifeless

ELITE (i-LEET) *noun* a group of people who have special advantages and privileges

EMPIRE (EM-pire) *noun* a group of countries or regions that have the same ruler

EPITAPH (EP-uh-taf) *noun* a short description of someone who has died

EXILED (EG-zih-uld) *adjective* sent away from one's homeland

FANATICISM (fuh-NAT-ih-sihz-um) *noun* extreme behavior caused by wild enthusiasm for an idea

IDEAL (eye-DEE-uhl) *noun* a standard of perfection

INTERVENE (in-tur-VEEN) *verb* to get involved in a situation in order to change how it ends up

INTOLERANCE (in-TOL-ur-inss) *noun* a lack of acceptance of other people

LEGACY (LEG-uh-see) *noun* something someone hands down to the next generation

MONARCH (MON-urk) *noun* a ruler who is in charge of a kingdom or an empire

PAWN (PAWN) *noun* a person used by others for their own purposes

PHILOSOPHER (fuh-LOSS-uh-fer) *noun* a person who studies what it means to be human

PROCURE (pruh-KYUR) *verb* to bring about or provide

PROPRIETY (pro-PRY-uh-tee) *noun* obedience to social rules

SUPERSTITION (soo-pur-STI-shuhn) *noun* the belief in magic, luck, or supernatural events

TYRANNICAL (ti-RAN-i-kuhl) *adjective* ruling others in a cruel or unjust way

INDEX

METRIC CONVERSIONS

Feet to meters: 1 ft is about 0.3 m
Miles to kilometers: 1 mi is about 1.6 km
Pounds to kilograms: 1 lb is about 0.45 kg